T0208893

LINDA CUTLER

WestBow Press books may be ordered through booksellers or by contacting:

WestBow Press
A Division of Thomas Nelson & Zondervan
1663 Liberty Drive
Bloomington, IN 47403
www.westbowpress.com
1 (866) 928-1240

ISBN: 978-1-9736-8398-8 (sc)
ISBN: 978-1-9736-8400-8 (hc)
ISBN: 978-1-9736-8399-5 (e)

Library of Congress Control Number: 2020901319

Print information available on the last page.

WestBow Press rev. date: 04/29/2020

This is dedicated to Carol, who inspired me to write this book and share my testimonies; Jackie, my Bible class instructor, who encouraged me; my friend Lisa, whose faith is strengthened; and my sons, Paul and Michael, for their strengths and beliefs.

Angels are with us and make appearances. I was raised Catholic but changed to Baptist and learned how to understand and apply the Bible to my life. What I will reveal to you is all true and, to me, very moving.

Angels are God's servants. There are good and bad angels. The bad ones used their free will to rebel. I will quote several Bible verses to support this truth. Hebrews 13:2 says, "Do not forget to entertain strangers, for by so doing some people have entertained angels without knowing it." Billy Graham and others state angels are mentioned in the Bible three hundred times. Luke 12:8–9 says, "I tell you whoever acknowledges Me before men, the son of man will also acknowledge him before the angels of God. But he who disowns Me before men will be disowned before the angels of God." Romans 8:38–39 says, "For I am convinced that neither death nor life, neither angels nor demons, neither the present nor the future, nor any powers, neither height nor depth, not anything else in all creation will be

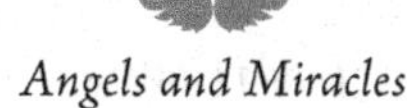

able to separate us from the love of God that is in Christ Jesus our Lord." Hebrews 1:14 says, "Are not all angels ministering spirits send to serve those who will inherit salvation? God testified through miracles according to His will." Another good one is Psalm 91:12, which says, "For He will command His angels concerning you to guard you in all your ways, they will life you up in their hands, so that you will not strike your foot against a stone."

I worked in retail as a cashier, and one day a lady came to my lane. Well, I know this may sound strange, but as I said, it is true. I felt she was not human. She wasn't scary but calming, and we had a nice conversation, which I cannot remember. All I do remember is that it was peaceful. I saw her walking away, and I turned to the other cashier and asked if she had seen the woman I had just checked out. I turned to watch her go, but she was already gone. It seemed too fast for her to have gotten to the door. The cashier looked strangely at me and replied, "Linda, there was no one there." I turned to the other cashier, asked the same thing, and got the same response.

I said, "Yes, there was. I rang her out and gave her the bag." I regrettably didn't think to ask security to check the camera. At the time, all I could think was, *Why didn't anyone else see her? I know what happened.* I discussed this with my pastor, and he said it could have been God or an angel. I think it was an angel. It is well with my soul.

My grandmother died when I was about eight years old. One night, my mother had told us of an experience she'd had after my grandmother's passing. She said she woke one night and felt a hand on hers. She thought it was one of us needing something. When she put on her eyeglasses and turned on the light, she saw her mother's image fading.

When I was sixteen, my dad passed away on Good Friday. I was the problem child, a rough, daring, and tough tomboy. My dad told me once that I was his favorite and should have been a boy. I would rather play baseball and basketball with the boys than play with dolls. My doll had no hair (because I cut it) and no clothes, and I think an arm was missing. I always had the knees worn out of my pants, and I had bruises—sliding into home base will do that. I was not very girly. Both of my sisters had perfectly dressed and groomed dolls. My two sisters and I slept in the same room at the top of the stairs. Every night we would go to bed, and later on, Dad would come up the steps. We would hear the chain on the bulb putting out the light and the doorknob turning, and then we would pretend

to be asleep. Well, about two nights after he was laid to rest, I heard his steps ascending on the stairs and whispered to my sisters, "Do you hear that?" They were sound asleep. Well, I heard the chain on the bulb and doorknob start to turn, and then I passed out.

When I told my mom in the morning, she asked why I hadn't opened the door. I didn't know. I was out cold. I always felt he came back to check on us one more time. I treasured that memory, and it was a remarkable experience.

My father was a fireman, and before bed, we would sit at the top of the stairs and listen to his work stories as he told my mother. We weren't allowed to do this, but we did anyway. After a few nights, we stopped. Every time I hear a fire truck's siren, I pray for those brave firefighters, knowing some of what they experience. I've been doing this since he went to heaven.

My mom started failing in health, and at that time she was in the Oklahoma Methodist Manor in Tulsa, Oklahoma. I flew out as soon as I heard. I found her removed from life support, as was planned. She was stiffening and unconscious but breathing. I put water on her lips and in her mouth and talked to her all day for a week. I was about to start a new job that week and explained to them my mother's situation. I was told they could hold the job for a week. Of course, I said I didn't know what would happen, but I agreed. I would spend all day reading the Bible, talking, and listening to the same Christian CD.

After a few days, you know what song came next. She didn't respond—she couldn't—but I felt she heard me. At the end of the week, I knew this was the end and told her that I would have to leave—and considering her condition, I would not return. I told her it was time to let go and be with Jesus. I said, "He's waiting for you." I kissed her head, said goodbye, and headed for the door.

Just before I got to the door, the CD skipped to the song "Blessed Assurance." *Wow,* was about all I could think. I got back to the motel and went to bed. At about 1:45 a.m., I awoke to her smell, not the nursing home smell. I turned, looked at the air, and said "Mom, is that you? Are you crossing over? Jesus is waiting. I'm glad you stopped by. Now, go on, and I'll see you when I get there." I remember watching the air. I saw nothing but followed a path with my eyes to the window. Then I put my head down and slept. About fifteen minutes later, I received a call from the nursing home saying she'd just passed and asking if I wanted to see her. I said no because she had just been here, and she was not there anymore.

Before I left, I went to get a few things of hers of sentimental value and her Last Supper plaque. I shared this with my pastor, who told me it was a wonderful thing to experience; few have that happen. The remarkable thing was I stayed at the same hotel every time I went to see her. This one last time, I changed my hotel and didn't tell anyone; it wasn't important. The call I received was about ten minutes after her passing. They were very lucky on the first try to reach me, considering there are many hotels/motels in Tulsa, and I had never stayed at that particular one before. Are we counting every blessing?

These experiences make me think deeper. I know heaven and angels exist. I also know God listens to prayers. These experiences have strengthened my belief and faith. The following are times that reinforced this for me. Our work gains meaning when it's done to honor God. We should enjoy our work; it's rewarding and all for His glory. There is joy in serving, which is what we are supposed to do. I have joy when folks return to let me know that God answered. That makes me want to do more. Even if I don't see or know the results of my requests and prayers, I have joy knowing

I served. It takes only a few minutes but can make quite a difference in people. To the world, you may be one person, but to that one person, you may be the world. Never give up.

For a long time, I worked in a factory doing repetitive work, and I developed carpal tunnel syndrome. Others experienced this condition, and surgery was recommended. The surgery did not guarantee to remedy the situation. I declined and had therapy. There was a coworker who had the surgery and was told she would have to have it done again. She saw me and asked if I'd had the surgery because I continued to work. I said I did not, but I prayed, and it went away. She looked at me unbelieving. I said to her, "What do you have to lose? Try it. God listened." This is another miracle.

In one home, I had an experience with seeing a black shape out of the corner of my eye. No matter how hard I tried, I could not see the entire vision. I called the Catholic Church and asked for a priest to cleanse the home. They came out and asked if I had a Ouija board. I said, "Yes, but I never use it. It's in the attic." I went to the attic where I was absolutely sure it was, but it wasn't there. I checked back several times, and eventually, there it was. Sanitation pickup was the next day, and out it went. The problems stopped. I was told it was a gateway to hell. No thanks, ever.

In another home where I lived with my younger son, I once heard footsteps and doors closing upstairs. I called, but he wasn't home; I was alone. The previous owners had left behind several cats. I could not keep them because my own cat wouldn't allow it. I put them outside, weather permitting, until I could take them to the shelter or find homes. I was inside, and there they were. I walked around the entire foundation, and there was no possible entry. I put them out again, and the same thing happened.

The basement had a small piece of sheetrock. One day I found two big knives, one a butcher and the other slightly smaller, in the sheetrock. I thought maybe my son was throwing knives. We had done this in the past for sport. He had not. I called the church again and asked for a cleansing, and they said, "Because it's the two of you, the large one might represent the bigger person, and the smaller knife might represent the smaller one." Fortunately the next day was sanitation pickup, and out they went.

I relocated to the South, which is the true Bible Belt. I'm still employed in retail and find it easy to pray for others. My Baptist church strengthens me, and I've come a long way in many ways. I'll begin with my experiences. Being Baptist has helped me raise my sons better and changed my life.

My son Michael helped me relocate to North Carolina and said I would need to replace the alternator in my car soon. I made an appointment for two days later. Well, work called that day and asked if I wanted to start. I did, the next day. I left work at about 6:00 p.m. and took the main road home instead of the back road. I got to the red light, and when it turned green, the car refused to proceed. I put the hood up and wondered what I would do. I didn't know anyone, it was going to be dark soon, and I was halfway home. I called a tow truck. Barbara pulled up behind me and asked if I needed help. I said I'd be fine, but at the time, I didn't believe what I was saying. I remember her saying she would give me a lift as long as I wasn't a serial killer. I hoped *she* wasn't one. She refused to leave me. I told her I didn't want to inconvenience her. My car was towed to the dealership. which was now closed, at about 7:00 p.m. What were the chances that there would be a man working late, and I could drop off my key? I told him I had an appointment the next day with them for the alternator. They called me and were sending a courtesy van, so I went outside to wait. I noticed my grass was cut! Jacki, my neighbor, had done it. Surprises! How good is God to watch out for me?

I transferred and kept my retail job, however they needed someone to work in the fitting room and answer the phone. A call came in from a hysterical young girl who desperately needed to speak to her brother because their father had been in a car accident. I immediately got him on the phone. Their father had been hit and was not breathing. They thought if he lived, he would have brain damage from lack of air to the brain.

I prayed so hard that night. This was just before Christmas. I was almost crying while I prayed because my dad had died on Good Friday, and every Easter was sad. I was mad at God for a long time. I was blessed to have the best father in the world. I didn't want this young man to spend every Christmas remembering sadness. I did understand and stopped being mad at God.

I saw the young man about a week later and asked how things were. He said, "You know, it's remarkable, but the doctors said there is no brain damage, and his body is healing at an unexplainable rate. Even the doctors are amazed."

That was when I got excited and said, "It's the power of prayer. Are you a Christian?" He said he was and believed. How amazing is that? Miracles continue to happen.

I went back to being a cashier. An opportunity arose when a lady told me what she was buying was for her sister, who was in the hospital. I asked if I could get her first name and pray for her. I didn't need to know what it was (and didn't want to pry because it could be upsetting), but God knew. She said, "Oh, would you, please?" Another miracle.

I saw her a few days later, and she said to me, "Do you remember me?" I said she looked familiar, but I was not sure from where I knew her. She said, "You prayed for my sister, and two days later, she was out of the hospital. Here she is." Wow, the power of prayer. I was just a messenger and had nothing to do with it. This was good work, and there was joy in serving. What do you have to lose? Think of all you have to gain! Faith, believing not seeing, and trusting is the way to go.

There are so many more times I've seen miracles. This man about twenty-five years old came to my register, and I was just about to leave for the day, so I put out the lane light as he arrived. He was walking like he had pain. I said, "Sorry, I'm about to punch out." I was only joking. He said okay. I said, "No, I'm only messing with you. Of course I'll ring you up."

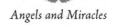

He said, "Thank you, because it would be painful to walk to another register. I'm having knee surgery tomorrow." I asked if I could pray for him. He was excited and said, "Please do."

As I always did, I wrote his first name on a piece of paper and put it in my pocket so that when I got home, I wouldn't forget. I told him, "I know prayer works, so when I see you next, I want to see you dancing." He said he would.

About a month passed, and this young man came up to me and asked if I remembered him. Again, I said I saw so many that I was not sure. He reminded me about the day we'd met. He said he remembered what I'd said, and he started dancing. I raised my hand and said, "Thank you, Jesus." He again asked if I would pray for him, for his surgery that Wednesday. I told him I wanted to see him do it again.

There was a time when I was a little short on the mortgage payment. I called work to ask if they had any extra hours. No, there weren't any hours. I put on my pajamas, feeling a bit depressed, and played my Christian music while I started washing the dishes. It was then that I raised my hands and said, "O God, this is in your hands."

Not ten minutes later, the phone rang, and work said an eight-hour shift had just opened up. They asked if I was still interested. Praise the Lord for that miracle!

All these happenings came from God, and they strengthened my faith. I pray that my example helps others as witnessing and testimony. It's what Jesus would do. I foreclosed my home and moved south. Well here was a miracle. God gives and takes away. What I left behind was impossible to sell. Nothing was impossible with God. He gave me a lovely home with land on the river, and it was off the beaten path. How blessed I was. It was more than I could imagine being blessed with, and I didn't deserve it.

Serving others should be our main concern. I was in a dollar store, and the young man in front of me was struggling with his change to pay for his socks. Struggle no more. I gave him what he needed and hoped that if it was my son, someone would do the same thing. Pay it forward, even if you don't receive now. It is said the least you do for a person, you do for God. He knows and listens; I am sure of that. Simple kindness is serving.

One day, a lady brutally complained to me about the self-checkout. I patiently listened and explained that there were positive sides as well because it sped up checking out. I didn't say anything negative; why add fuel to the fire? At the end, she remarked that she felt bad and apologized about her ranting. I said I didn't even notice and hoped she had a good day. She left in a better mood, smiling.

This is written to say that we all have opportunities; some we find, and others find us. Pursuing and helping to strengthen and encourage others should be our concern. Nothing you do for God goes unnoticed. It's rewarding to see these miracles, however, even if you don't you know, you put it out there and pray for others.

God provides even the small things. One day, I wanted a BLT. I put tomatoes as my first item on shopping list. Sure enough, I got home and had everything but the tomatoes. I went to sit outside for a few moments, pondering the crazy thought of driving to the store for a tomato. Just then, my neighbor came over and asked if I could use some tomatoes. Wow!

One day, I was driving with my sons, and a motorcycle had broken down in front of us. I stopped to help him. We got him going on his way, and at the next block, we got a flat tire. I'd like to think this was a miracle saving us; perhaps we were saved by an accident up ahead had we proceeded. I like to think this was an angel protecting us.

Another time, I had a coworker who was very rude, telling me things that I did about the job in which I was still training. I said nothing and let her go on and on. Another coworker Vicki heard it all and said to me, "You didn't come back and defend yourself or get upset." Again, why add fuel to the fire? Perhaps she needed to vent and chose me to do so. I was from New York, so I'm sure I could have torn her up, but why? It's not where you are from; it's what you are made of. The coworker who observed this said to me, "She was being very difficult, but you handled it sweetly."

That Sunday, the church sermon was about how to deal with difficult people. I think the Lord smiled on me because I'd done the right thing. Sounds like well done to me, and with approval. What would Jesus do? I turned the other cheek. That reinforced my faith and attitude. Of course, we all get disturbed over situations like this, but it's how we handle them that defines us. If someone hates you, show love and forgiveness with understanding. I went to work and told the coworker who'd witnessed the incident what the sermon was about. She smiled. God can reach you if you are open to listen. How great is our God? I like the expression "Without Jesus, it's hell."

This prayer warrior that I've become has gotten around. One of my coworkers asked if I could pray for her father because doctors think cancer showed up on the biopsy, and they wanted to do another biopsy. She heard me pray for others and always remark, "God's at work."

I prayed, and later on, she said, "Now the doctors can't find it." They thought something wrong and wanted to do a third biopsy. Same results: clean. How awesome. She asked me to pray for her dog. I said I would. Then she asked me to pray for her daughter, which I did.

I met a friend from another Baptist church Kim and told her all I'd seen and tried, adding that I hadn't gotten an answer on this one and didn't understand. She reminded me I did. The answer was to wait. I forgot about that answer because I didn't like to wait. "Learn patience, my child." Yes, Lord, give me patience—but hurry up.

In Hebrews 1:14, we are told that angels are sent to do for us what they did for Jesus. They strengthen us in our hour of need. The primary function of angels is to be messengers;

their appearance is likely to be suited to the occasion or the recipient of the message. The fact that angels are among us compels us to be kind and loving to everyone regardless of who we think they are.

A man came in to the store, and I greeted him and asked him how he was. His answer was, "I'm fine but have hand surgery scheduled for next week. This was thrust on me."

I turned to him to speak only to him; I didn't think anyone could hear me. The lady behind him was not that close but asked me if I could pray for her aunt. Wow, opportunities are given. Take them, use them, work it, and serve.

I asked one lady who was in a wheelchair how she was doing, and she opened up immediately about her difficult trouble with finances and getting aid. I didn't even get a chance to ask. I asked if I could pray for her, and she said she was not religious but spiritual. I said, "I've seen miracles, and God will listen and answer. God is spiritual and listening; believe and trust in Him." Her attitude softened as if she considered what I said.

One time, I worked the fitting room. A lady simply pulled down her blouse to show me the scar from surgery so she could find something appropriate to wear. I invited her to my church and of course put her on the prayer list. So many times I've been talking to people who simply open up and start telling me their situations. I wonder whether God sends them to me, and they feel comfortable enough to talk to me about personal situations. Being in the right place at the right time is joy. I think God has me where He wants me to be. I can do all things through God, who strengthens me, and that's amazing grace. I am grateful to do the work He allows.

I was diagnosed with a brain tumor about ten years ago. I thought I was going to die. The procedure went horribly wrong. They put a cap on my head to go through the radiation. They apparently put it too tight because it cracked my skull, and I had brain fluid running out of my nose. While my shirt and shoes were wet from the drip, I returned to ask what was going on. Then I asked, "How much fluid can I lose before I die?" They said it was about half a can of soda. How professional a measurement was that? I said, "I'm up to about half now, so now what?" It should close itself, they claimed.

"When?" I wondered. I had to have tapes and sponges put in my nose to absorb the fluid. My sons came to visit, and they asked what was on my face because the tape held the sponges. I said it was sinus, because I've always had severe sinus problems that specialists could not repair. As the drip continued, a natural reflex was to suck it in, and that pulled the sponges down my throat. I returned to the hospital, and all I got was annoyance at what I had done as they replaced the sponges. "Hey, I'm the one suffering, really." Some bedside manner experience! I did research to find out what to do and learned that I was the thirteenth person in the United States to experience this. That was when I did no more research because none survived. I was told to return for a checkup. "Do you really think I will return after what you did?" I asked if it was cancerous and was told it didn't matter because the radiation would have taken care of it. Why would I return? God is the best physician. They said the tumor could grow, stay the same, or shrink. "Excuse me, but I have some brain cells left, and I think I can see those as the options." I never returned and am fine. I think God saved me.

The interesting punchline here is I was going to a Baptist church with my pastor's son, with whom I worked. I somewhat recovered and went to church, and the pastor said we should pray for a young man who graduated MIT with high honors and had a fiancée and a bright future. At about age twenty-three, he was diagnosed with a brain tumor and passed in days. I looked at my friend and asked him why God would take this boy, who had such a future, yet leave an old lady like me? I was fifty at the time. He said, "God has plans for you and work for you to do." In the last four years, I've seen this is true. I have worked toward helping and praying for others. He has changed my life, and I see it and am so grateful. I feel His strength and trust. This is amazing that I can do what I am. I'm not patting myself on the back at all. What I do, I do for God, and I'm so glad he allows me to do this work, which I enjoy.

I saw this lady and her son. It appeared he was a little slow, but it was not very noticeable. He was a pleasure to talk to as he greeted me happily and loudly, not shy at all. He took the purchases out to the car, and I said it was a pleasure to meet him before he left. He was with his mother, and I told her what a lovely young son she had. She told me he had been in an accident with resulting brain damage. I decided to tell her about my brain tumor and how God had given me a miracle. I told her how much I believed change could happen, because I'd seen it, regardless of the seriousness of the situation. I prayed for him the next few nights.

It's painful to see so much hurting in the world, but I keep praying. People appreciate my concern and sincerity.

I have met many others who simply start telling me of their upcoming surgery or difficulties. It's incredible how they are in my path. We have to be survivors and heroes in faith, and strength will grow. I don't get the chance to talk to some of them, but what I see hurts, and I pray for them. God knows who they are and the situation, so I simply talk to God.

One of my sons, Michael, came to visit on his motorcycle. It was time for him to return home, and he was hot-wiring the bike. I knew what he was doing but asked anyway. He said he couldn't find the key. Now, this was ugly because he had a twelve-hour trip in the rain. I put up my hands and said, "Please, God, help us find the keys."

My son said, "Oh, yeah, like He's just going to throw them on the couch." I said I didn't know, but we should go inside and find out. We'd already searched and hadn't found them. We went inside, and there they were, on the floor by the couch.

We went back outside, and he was unwiring as I raised my hands and said, "Thank you, Jesus."

My neighbor came over and said to my son, "This is no joke. Your mama prayed for her dog last Christmas when he was hit by a car. The dog was paralyzed for about a day. I said it could be trauma, and I prayed. I was hit by a car when I was a pedestrian at about age sixteen, and I couldn't walk for about two days. It was trauma, a shock to my spinal system, and then I started walking. The next day, the dog started walking. Miracles do happen, and as stated previously, it's God decision to reverse conditions, prove doctors wrong, and do His miracles. By seeing these miracles, my faith has become stronger, and even the ones I don't see, because it's all in His hands. All I can do, as we all should, is ask and be patient with prayer."

My other son, Paul, called me when his car broke down. He had to meet the tow truck, so he returned there on his motorcycle. Well, the tow truck was late in coming, and it started to rain as it got dark. I told him to keep praying, and he said the more he did, the worse it got because he had now lost his wallet. I said it was the devil coming at him, and he should resist and pray, as I was. The situation improved, and he got home safely even though he was unfamiliar with the road and the weather was not in his favor. His wallet was returned. Prayer answered.

A lady and her mother came to check out, and I asked how they were. One said she was fine but had just gotten out of the hospital. Sometimes I ask why, and sometimes I simply ask if they are okay. This time I asked why. She pulled up her blouse to show me an enormous scar that ran the length of her midsection, and it was a crooked line. She said it went horribly bad. I told her that at least she was standing here and recovering. I told her to use vitamin E cream that would diminish scarring but not eliminate it. I asked if I could pray for her. She agreed, and I did so. It was then that I told her about my brain tumor surgery that had gone horribly bad as well, but I was still here and fine. She left looking a bit better.

I was working as a cashier and talking to a man who asked me where I was originally from. I told him and remarked that I had had a difficult time being a Baptist up north. We talked some more, and the man behind him was listening. He asked if I was a Baptist, and I said I'd been a strong one for a long time. He introduced himself as a Baptist minister and told me to keep doing what I did.

I was to have major plumbing repairs, and the plumber didn't show up three times. One of the times, I called, and he didn't get a chance to call me. The day after the third no-show, I went home, raised one hand to God, and said, "I'm not dealing with this. I'm done for today." I put on my Christian music. Not one minute later, he pulled into my driveway.

This was a day I'll always remember. This lady and four young girls came in, and one of the young girls was holding the buggy the entire time, looking down. I felt something was wrong. I didn't get much chance to interact with them because they kept their eyes down. As they were leaving, the pretty girl who was holding the buggy walked like she had (I guessed) cerebral palsy. This touched my heart as I watched her painful steps. I began praying silently for her. I asked God to find mercy to straighten her legs and help her, because she was so young. I was emotionally touched and felt sad. I was near tears. I turned to the next customer, a young man, and asked how he was. He replied he was fine. When I handed him his change, our eye contact was amazing. I knew what I felt. My feet felt like they were pulled to the spot where I was standing. I was frozen in place as I looked into his eyes. They were greenish-blue and conveyed such a peace. This lasted a few seconds, enough to make me feel differently about him. All I could think was, *Wow, he looks like the Jesus that I know from movies and pictures.*

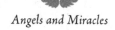

He clearly and slowly said "God bless you." Wow, I felt that God was reinforcing what I had just done in silence, praying for that girl. I felt this because it was immediately after she left. I wished him a blessed day and thought about that moment all day.

I talked to my Sunday school teacher, Jackie, that night. I couldn't stop wondering whether it was Jesus or an angel. I've been called a religious fanatic, but I'm not crazy. I do have some brain cells left. She told me Jesus doesn't come back in human form to us, but He sends His angels. I believe this was an encounter. It was the second time in my life, and I knew this was a different meeting than with a person. How amazing and strengthening. I think the message to me was to keep going, and I will.

Some days I meet so many who need prayers that I feel worn out when I get on my knees to pray. I follow up on some. I sleep well when worn out because I keep my word. Sometimes I wonder what would have happened if I was not bold enough to ask to pray for those in need. I told God one night that I was.

There are so many times we have opportunities. I experience a lot of them and am forever changed by what I see happening.

I have very loud tree frogs. A repairman came over about five in the afternoon, and they started up. He remarked he'd never heard them that loud. I told him, "Come back in three hours when there are hundreds of them." I went to get buckshot because it was bad. The man asked me how I slept, and I answered, "Not well."

The man at the store asked if I wanted to quiet them or rid myself of them. He said they were itty-bitty things.

I said, "Nope, they are stuck to my screen door and are about two inches or so." I didn't want to do this but when you can't sleep, it is difficult. I was going to bed, and they were loud that before I put my head on the pillow, I asked God to make them quiet or go away. As soon as my head hit the pillow, there was silence. This is true!

Before I turned Baptist, I had a bad motorcycle accident and broke my arm. The bone fragments were like a bag of chips given the way I was hit by a hit-and-run driver. Doctors said they would have to amputate because there was nothing to piece together.

I refused, but rebreaking and resetting the cast was off. Doctors said it was a useless limb and could barely get 10 percent usage. I didn't give up, and with therapy, I got to 100 percent usage. By the way, I was about twenty years old at the time and refused to go through life as they had predicted. Miracles happen.

One day, I was on a break from work and sat outside on the bench. A man came along and asked if he could join me. I said of course. We started talking about motorcycles, and he invited me to his biker church. It was great, and I've been a few times. To look at all 5'2",

100 pounds of me, one would never know, but I taught myself to ride when I was twelve and rode for a lifetime; my sons also ride. I wanted to share that angels show up in mysterious places and times.

At work, a man was buying Harley Davidson gift cards, so I asked him if he rode. He said no, but his dad did. I handed him a token with the biker church logo and information, and he was so grateful that he hugged me. He said his dad was looking for a biker church. It was amazing how these special moments arise and are answered. Perhaps I'm in the right place and at the right time. It is said that God puts you where he wants you. I can see that happening.

We all have opportunities to help each other with kindness. This is the serving that we need to do. It is returned to us without looking for it, even with simple, silent prayers. Asking to pray for others you see in need reinforces and strengthens it, and it is wonderful testimony to others. By the way, when I've asked to pray for people, sometimes they add to my list and ask me to pray for someone else. Others overhear and also ask me. I am blessed to have such opportunities, and I take advantage of them. God hears all these requests and answers in His own way and His own time. Patience is difficult, but wait for the answer.

God uses us by our example to change unbelievers' hearts or strengthen others. We can be assured of God being with us every step of the way, providing for our needs. We are to love and serve unconditionally by putting others' needs ahead of our own. It's challenging at times to follow the Lord's example, but it can be done. I know I am not who I used to be.

This is being written so that we can examine ourselves and determine whether we are doing all we can. It's important to our character and setting an example.

A memorable day was when an elderly couple came to me. The lady handed me some little silver crosses, and I thanked her. I went to dinner and sat next to a lady. I really wanted to sit farther down but chose that place. As I was getting ready to leave, she told the server that she'd had a stroke and possibly lost her vision in that eye, and her husband was recovering from cancer. Well, of course I gave her one of the crosses and got their names so I could pray for them that night. About a week later, in came the elderly couple. I recognized them but did not remember from where I might know them. She came up to me and handed me some crosses. I said, "Now I know you." I told her I'd given them out and had appreciated them. I asked for their names so I could pray for them. She told me their names: Mary and Joseph. All I could say was, "Wow."

David Jeremiah said, "Angels are extensions of God's love, care, grace and guidance upon our lives even when we're unaware of their presence." He said angels are mentioned seventy-two times in Revelation alone. Dark angels joined Satan in rebellion against God.

Can you recall a moment in your life when you felt you had been protected or given supernatural help?

I've been reading much about angels, demons, and choices. A child has some genes from the parents that provide the child's demeanor. This can be changed through conditioning, learning, and experiences. I've seen where things can change. Let's positively influence children one at a time. "The least you do for them, you do for Me," God said. Set examples that will be copied and admired. If a child is brought up in a home where there is no structure as to behavior, this can change with maturity. Experiences of relating to others and the environment are crucial to knowing rights and wrongs. How we are hurt can hurt others, and we should know the difference and adapt. If someone wrongs you and hurts you, is it the bad angel on your shoulder who encourages you to retaliate? Knock it off and accept the good angel on your other shoulder. This can be taught, however not everyone accepts this idea. Dealing with others in a kind way is the key. If one wrongs you, do not retaliate; God is the only judge. This is difficult. As a child, I was defensive, but I changed my ways, and now I forgive and let it go. It takes work and trusting God to help. I learned to put all in God's hands. He has big hands, apparently, because I know I filled them for sure.

I live in North Carolina, and there are snakes. I had a pile of cardboard I was going to burn, and instead of picking it all up at once, I decided to take one piece at a time. This was most likely an angel at my side because when I picked up the top one, there was a copperhead. I knew I was protected at that moment. Angels have to be real.

You don't have a promise of tomorrow, so make your deeds count today. It doesn't matter what you've done because you are never too far gone to ask forgiveness and trust Him.

This may sound odd, but I think domesticated animals are like angels. It is said they don't have souls, but I believe they go to heaven because God loves them. They don't know right from wrong—or is that so? When my pets did something not pleasing to me, they immediately realized it and would put their heads down in guilt. I believe we all have an inner feeling when a deed is not acceptable, and I believe animals experience this. If they do a bad deed and feel badly, is that realizing right from wrong? They cannot communicate in our language, but they understand us. So how can it be proved that animals do not have a connection to God? They are our angel-like companions. When I came home with a broken foot and entered the doorway, immediately my cat and dog were at the door. They both looked at my face and then down at my foot. How could they know? They comfort us as angels when we are sad. They know our feelings. So will they be in heaven? I believe so. God gave us animals for companions. They protect us as angels do.

All dogs go to heaven, as do all good pets. These animals have instincts. The unreasoning animals, the wild animals who are not domesticated and simply live to survive, do not. I read a quote by the late Billy Graham: "It may be God's purpose for animals is fulfilled on this earth. However, if animals would make us happier in heaven, surely there will be a place for them there." The Holy Spirit, who comforts us in other losses in life, will bring comfort when we lose our animals. We have a Father who cares for every part of our lives, including our pets, which are family. This I believe.

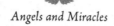

My Animal Hospital has a sign outside "Animals are like little angels sent to earth to teach us how to love.

I've tried to do the best I could and look forward (as we all should) to God saying, "Well done."

Printed in the United States
By Bookmasters